The Carlisle Indian School

by Amanda Turner

PEARSON

Glenview, Illinois • Boston, Massachusetts • Chandler, Arizona
Upper Saddle River, New Jersey

Native American land is in purple. Native Americans lost a lot of land from 1850 to 1890.

Land Is Lost

Long ago, Native Americans were the first people to live in North America. Many lived in the West.

In the 1600s and 1700s, white settlers came. In the 1850s, they moved into the West.

The settlers took land from Native Americans. The U.S. Army fought Native Americans. The government made them leave their land.

Captain Richard Pratt

Captain Pratt's Idea

The government sent Native Americans away. They sent them to reservations to live. Some people thought the Native Americans would fight. So one man had an idea.

Richard Pratt was a captain in the army. He wanted Native American children to be like white children. He wanted to send them to boarding school. Children live at boarding schools.

Chief Spotted Tail

Captain Pratt made a boarding school. He called it the Carlisle Indian School. It was in Carlisle, Pennsylvania.

Captain Pratt then met with Lakota Sioux chiefs. Chiefs are leaders. Chief Spotted Tail was the Lakota leader. He did not trust Captain Pratt. He did not want white people to teach Lakota children.

Native American children learned many things at home.

Pratt Wins

Captain Pratt told Chief Spotted Tail about the school. He said the children would learn English. They would learn to read and write.

The Lakota chiefs did not want their children to leave. But the chiefs wanted a better life for the children. Finally, the chiefs agreed.

The Lakota were the first children at the school. From 1879 to 1918, other groups sent their children there too.

A Native American before (left) and after (right) his time at Carlisle School

First Days at School

School was hard for the children. They missed their homes. They had to make big changes.

The children wore new kinds of clothes. They wore shoes. Boys' long hair was cut short. Teachers gave them English names. These new names were hard to say. The children learned new ways to eat. Everything changed for them.

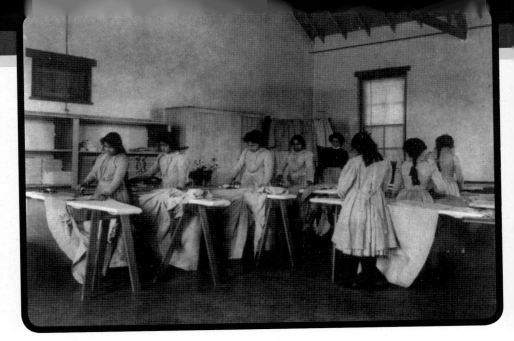

Girls working at the Carlisle School

Life at School

Life at school was like being in the army. Children slept together in big rooms. They marched to class. The boys dressed like soldiers.

Children had to work hard there. Girls cleaned and cooked. Boys farmed. They cared for animals. They also built new buildings.

Conclusion

Life at the Carlisle School was hard. Children missed their families. Some got sick and died.

After the school, some children did not go home. They kept their English names. They wore white people's clothes. Some did go home, though. They wanted to live with their Lakota families.